T0298994

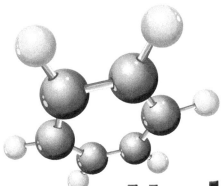

Understanding Physical & Chemical Changes

An Interactive Discovery-Based Science Unit for High-Ability Learners

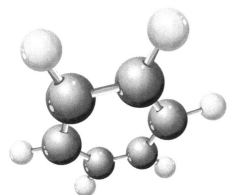

Grades 6-8

Understanding Physical & Chemical Changes

Richard G. Cote & Darcy O. Blauvelt

Routledge
Taylor & Francis Group

NEW YORK AND LONDON

First published 2012 by Prufrock Press Inc.

Published 2021 by Routledge
605 Third Avenue, New York, NY 10017
2 Park Square, Milton Park, Abingdon, Oxon OX14 4RN

Routledge is an imprint of the Taylor & Francis Group, an informa business

Copyright © 2012 by Taylor & Francis.

Edited by Sarah Morrison

Production design by Raquel Trevino

ISBN 13: 978-1-59363-831-3 (pbk)

Table of Contents

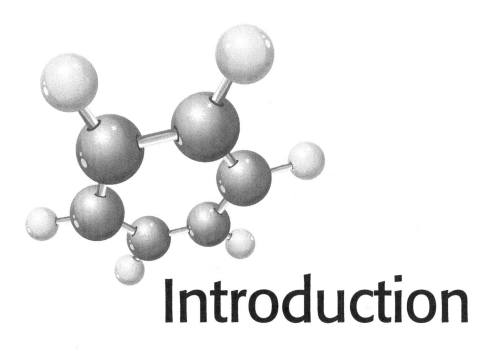

Introduction

Background

Gifted program directors, resource specialists, and—perhaps most importantly—general education classroom teachers who struggle with the challenge of providing appropriate services to students of high potential in the traditional classroom will be interested in these Interactive Discovery-Based Units for High-Ability Learners. The units encourage students to use nontraditional methods to demonstrate learning.

Any given curriculum is composed of two distinct, though not separate, entities: content and context. In every classroom environment, there are forces at work that define the content to be taught. These forces may take the form of high-stakes tests or local standards. But in these Interactive Discovery-Based Units for High-Ability Learners, the context of a traditional classroom is reconfigured so that students are provided with a platform from which to demonstrate academic performance and understanding that are not shown through traditional paper-and-pencil methods. This way, teachers go home smiling and students go home tired at the end of the school day.

C = C + C
Curriculum = Content + Context

In March of 2005, the Further Steps Forward Project (FSFP) was established and funded under the Jacob K. Javits Gifted and Talented Students Education Program legislation. The project had a two-fold, long-range mission:

- The first goal was to identify, develop, and test identification instruments specific to special populations of the gifted, focusing on the economically disadvantaged.
- The second goal was to create, deliver, and promote professional development focused on minority and underserved populations of the gifted, especially the economically disadvantaged.

The result was the Student Context Rubric (SCR), which is included in each of the series' eight units. The SCR, discussed in further depth in the Appendix, is a rubric that a teacher or specialist uses to evaluate a student in five areas: engagement, creativity, synthesis, interpersonal ability, and verbal communication. When used in conjunction with the units in this series, the SCR provides specialists with an excellent tool for identifying students of masked potential—students who are gifted but are not usually recognized—and it gives general education teachers the language necessary to advocate for these students when making recommendations for gifted and additional services. The SCR also provides any teacher with a tool for monitoring and better understanding student behaviors.

Using best practices from the field of gifted education as a backdrop, we viewed students through the lens of the following core beliefs as we developed each unit:

- instrumentation must be flexible in order to recognize a variety of potentials;
- curricula must exist that benefit all students while also making clear which students would benefit from additional services; and
- identification processes and services provided by gifted programming must be integral to the existing curriculum; general education teachers cannot view interventions and advocacy as optional.

These eight contextually grounded units, two in each of the four core content areas (language arts, social studies, math, and science), were developed to serve as platforms from which middle school students could strut their stuff, displaying their knowledge and learning in practical, fun contexts. Four of the units (*Ecopolis*, *Mathematics in the Marketplace*, *Order in the Court*, and *What's Your Opinion?*) have been awarded the prestigious National Association for Gifted Children (NAGC) Curriculum Award. Over the span of 3 years, we—and other general education teachers—taught all of the units multiple times to measure their effectiveness as educational vehicles and to facilitate dynamic professional development experiences.

The FSFP documented that in 11 of 12 cases piloted in the 2008–2009 school year, middle school students showed statistically significant academic gains. In particular, those students who were underperforming in the classroom showed great progress. Furthermore, there were statistically significant improvements in students' perceptions of their classroom environments in terms of innovation and involvement. Finally, the contextually grounded units in this series can be used as springboards for further study and projects, offering teachers opportunities for cross-disciplinary collaboration.

Administrators, teachers, and gifted specialists will gain from this series a better sense of how to develop and use contextualized units—not only in the regular education classroom, but also in gifted programming.

How to Use the Units

Every lesson in the units includes an introductory section listing the concepts covered, suggested materials, grade-level expectations, and student objectives. This section also explains how the lesson is introduced, how students demonstrate recognition of the concepts, how they apply their knowledge, and how they solve related problems. The lesson plans provided, while thorough, also allow for differentiation and adaptation. Depending on how much introduction and review of the material students need, you may find that some lessons take more or less time than described. We have used these units in 50-minute class periods, but the subparts of the lesson—introducing the material, recognizing the concepts, applying knowledge, and solving a problem—allow for adaptability in terms of scheduling. The "Additional Notes" for each lesson provide further tips, flag potential problem areas, and offer suggestions for extending the lesson.

This series offers many contextual units from which to choose; however, we do not recommend using them exclusively. In our research, we have found that students who are constantly involved in contextual learning become immune to its benefits. We recommend, therefore, that you vary the delivery style of material across the school year. For most classes, spacing out three contextual units over the course of the year produces optimal results.

These units may be used in place of other curriculum. However, if you find that your students are stumbling over a specific skill as they progress through a unit, do not hesitate to take a day off from the unit and instead use direct instruction to teach that skill. (For instance, in this unit, you may pause the unit for some direct instruction regarding the scientific method.) This will help to ensure that students are successful as they move forward. It is necessary for students to be frustrated and challenged, as this frustration serves as the impetus of learning—yet they must not be so frustrated that they give up. Throughout the unit, you must find the delicate balance between providing challenges for your students and overwhelming them.

The Role of the Teacher

A contextual unit is a useful vehicle both for engaging your students and for assessing their abilities. As a teacher, your role changes in a contextual unit. Rather than being the driving force, you are the behind-the-scenes producer. The students are the drivers of this creative vehicle. If you are used to direct instruction methods of teaching, you will need to make a conscious choice not to run the show. Although this may feel a bit uncomfortable for you in the beginning, the rewards for your students will prove well worth the effort. As you become more comfortable with the process, you will find that this teaching method is conducive to heightening student engagement and learning while also allowing you to step back and observe your students at work.

Group Dynamics

Cooperation plays a key role in this unit. Small-group work is fraught with challenges for all of us. Creating groups that will be able to accomplish their objectives—groups whose members will fulfill their roles—takes some forethought. Keep in mind that sometimes the very act of working through any issues that arise may be the most powerful learning tool of all. Before beginning the unit, you should discuss with students the importance of working together and assigning tasks to ensure that work is distributed and completed fairly and equally.

Preparation and Pacing

Deciding on a timeline is very important as you plan the implementation of the unit. You know your students better than anyone else does. Some students may be more successful when they are immersed in the unit, running it every day for 3 weeks. Others would benefit from having some days off to get the most out of their experiences.

Every classroom is different. Students possess different sets of prior knowledge, learning strategies, and patterns. This means that as the teacher, you must make decisions about how much of the material you will introduce prior to the unit, whether you will provide occasional traditional instruction throughout the unit, how many days off you will give students, and how much your students will discover on their own throughout the course of the unit. For example, in this science unit, students perform a series of experiments to experience the differences between physical and chemical changes. You may choose to teach these concepts prior to using the unit, and then use the unit to replace the practice days that would usually follow. Another option is to use the unit without preteaching these concepts, instead allowing the unit's activities to show which students already possess some content knowledge and which students are experiencing more difficulty. If you choose the latter option, it is important to use the pretest carefully and to cultivate an encouraging atmosphere in the classroom. The pretest is somewhat unconventional, as students are prompted simply to write everything that they know about physical and chemical changes. This intentional open-ended preassessment allows students a wider than usual opportunity to demonstrate any levels of scientific thinking (observe, organize, infer, and predict) they may possess at the outset of the unit. The optional lesson covers this type of scientific thinking in more depth. As an end-of-unit assessment, students will be asked to generate visual aids and develop a presentation in addition to writing. This book is not meant to provide exact instructions; in every lesson, there is wiggle room in terms of how you work alongside students to enable them to demonstrate learning.

Also, you should feel free to use materials other than those suggested. If there is a topic or source that is highly relevant for your students, then it might be worthwhile for you to compile research sites, articles, and other materials about the topic in order to provide your students a degree of real-world involvement.

Using these units is a bit like using a recipe in the kitchen. The first time you use one of the units, you may want to use it just as it is written. Each successive time you use it, however, you may choose to adjust the ratios and substitute ingredients to suit your own tastes. The more you personalize the units to your students' situations and preferences, the more engaged they will be—and the same goes for you as the teacher.

Next Generation Science Standards and Common Core State Standards

This unit is aligned with the Next Generation Science Standards (NGSS) and the Common Core State Standards (CCSS) for English-Language Arts-Literacy and we hope that will be helpful to you. Rather than listing the relevant standards with each lesson (as we have in previous books), we are providing a comprehensive list (below) of the standards addressed by the lessons in this unit, as once the students begin the experimentation process the standards are the same for every lesson. Thus, within the NGSS cluster of Middle School: Matter and Its Interactions, the students will meet the following standards:

- MS-PS1-1. Develop models to describe the atomic composition of simple molecules and extended structures.

- MS-PS1-2. Analyze and interpret data on the properties of substances before and after the substances interact to determine if a chemical reaction has occurred.
- MS-PS1-4. Develop a model that predicts and describes changes in particle motion, temperature, and state of a pure substance when thermal energy is added or removed.
- MS-PS1-5. Develop and use a model to describe how the total number of atoms does not change in a chemical reaction and thus mass is conserved.
- MS-PS1-6. Undertake a design project to construct, test, and modify a device that either releases or absorbs thermal energy by chemical processes.

Within the NGSS cluster of Middle School: Engineering Design, the students will meet the following standards:
- MS-ETS1-1. Define the criteria and constraints of a design problem with sufficient precision to ensure a successful solution, taking into account relevant scientific principles and potential impacts on people and the natural environment that may limit possible solutions.
- MS-ETS1-2. Evaluate competing design solutions using a systematic process to determine how well they meet the criteria and constraints of the problem.
- MS-ETS1-3. Analyze data from tests to determine similarities and differences among several design solutions to identify the best characteristics of each that can be combined into a new solution to better meet the criteria for success.
- MS-ETS1-4. Develop a model to generate data for iterative testing and modification of a proposed object, tool, or process such that an optimal design can be achieved.

Additionally, the lessons meet the following standards for the CCSS ELA-Literacy cluster of Literacy in Science/Technical Subjects for Grades 6–8:
- RST.6-8.2 Determine the central ideas or conclusions of a text; provide an accurate summary of the text distinct from prior knowledge or opinions.
- RST.6-8.3 Follow precisely a multistep procedure when carrying out experiments, taking measurements, or performing technical tasks.
- RST.6-8.5 Analyze the structure an author uses to organize a text, including how the major sections contribute to the whole and to an understanding of the topic.
- RST.6-8.6 Analyze the author's purpose in providing an explanation, describing a procedure, or discussing an experiment in a text.
- RST.6-8.8 Distinguish among facts, reasoned judgment based on research findings, and speculation in a text.
- RST.6-8.9 Compare and contrast the information gained from experiments, simulations, video, or multimedia sources with that gained from reading a text on the same topic.

Adaptability

"Organized chaos" is a phrase often used to describe a contextual classroom. The students are not sitting at their desks and quietly taking notes while the teacher delivers information verbally. A classroom full of students actively engaged in their learning and creatively solving real-world problems is messy, but highly productive. Every teacher has his or her own level of tolerance for this type of chaos, and you may find yourself needing days off occasionally. Organization is an essential ingredient for success in a contextual unit. For example, you will need a place in your classroom where students can access paperwork. It is important to think through timeframes and allow for regular debriefing sessions.

You will also want to develop a personalized method for keeping track of who is doing what. Some students will be engaged from the start, but others you will need to prod and encourage to become involved. This will be especially true if your students are unfamiliar with this type of contextual learning. There are always a few students who try to become invisible so that classmates will do their work for them. Others may be Tom Sawyers, demonstrating their interpersonal skills by persuading peers to complete their work. You will want to keep tabs on both of these types of students so that you can maximize individual student learning. Some teachers have students keep journals, others use daily exit card strategies, and others use checklists. Again, many aspects of how to use these units are up to you.

It is difficult in a busy classroom to collect detailed behavioral data about your students, but one advantage of contextual learning is that it is much easier to spend observation time in the classroom when you are not directly running the show! If you have the luxury of having an assistant or classroom visitor who can help you collect anecdotal data, then we recommend keeping some sort of log of student behavior. What has worked well for us has been to create a list of students' pictures, with a blank box next to each picture in which behaviors can be recorded.

Contextual units require the teacher to do a considerable amount of work prior to beginning the unit, but once you have put everything into place, the students take over and you can step back and observe as they work, solve problems, and learn.

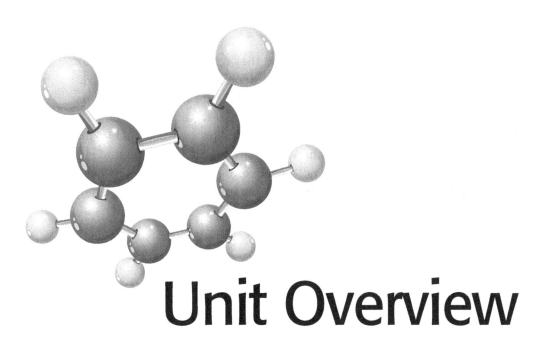

Unit Overview

This unit and accompanying rubric were designed to assess the degree to which students understand and are able to apply the concepts of physical and chemical change, as well as students' ability to think scientifically.

The unit is intended to challenge all students. It begins by working with the concepts and definitions of physical and chemical change while paying particular attention to the indicators of those changes. Students are encouraged to develop data collection tables to use in the experimental phase. Moving through a series of lab stations, students conduct simple experiments while making qualitative and quantitative observations. After organizing their findings, they present their results to the class, readying students to become experiment designers. (They will use their presentation skills again after designing and conducting their own experiments.) In a summative authentic performance assessment, each lab team designs two original experiments (one to demonstrate a physical change, and one to demonstrate a chemical change) that illustrates the concepts they have learned. The students set up their experiments, materials, and instructions to enable other lab teams to conduct their experiments, and data are collected.

Each lesson is organized into four components: introduction, recognition, application, and problem solving. The teacher introduces the concept. Then, students are given the opportunity to demonstrate that they recognize the concept, can apply the concept, and can solve a problem using the concept. Using this organizational tool gives the teacher greater latitude in differentiating each lesson based on students' prior knowledge, skills, levels of engagement, and readiness.

Additionally, we have included an optional lesson entitled "Thinking Scientifically." In our experience, this lesson will be particularly useful for students who have not received training or have not been exposed to the rigors of making formal qualitative or quantitative observations, organizing data, drawing inferences, or making predictions.

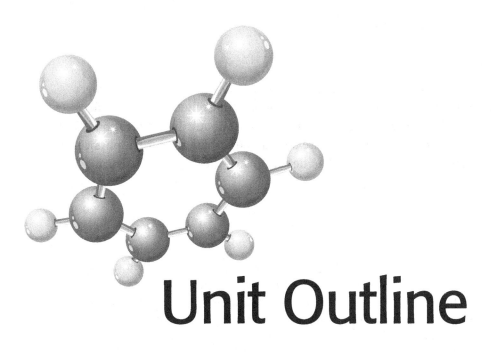

Unit Outline

We designed these lessons to be used during 50-minute class periods. Depending on the extent to which you need to review concepts with your students and the amount of time you decide to devote to particular activities, some of these lessons may take fewer or more days than indicated. We have noted approximately how many days each lesson will take to complete.

Optional Lesson: Thinking Scientifically

Many students have difficulty with the process of scientific thought, particularly with respect to making detailed observations. In order to sharpen students' understanding, teachers may find it advantageous to use this optional lesson. It is designed to expose students to making qualitative and quantitative observations, organizing data, drawing inferences from those data, and making predictions about future events. (*Note*: This lesson requires 2 days.)

Lesson 1

Students demonstrate their prior knowledge of physical and chemical changes by completing a short writing challenge of the Type I John Collins style. After sharing student descriptions, the teacher leads a discussion about the implications of physical and chemical changes. Students are taught and discuss the terms "physical change" and "chemical change," as well as definitions of the indicators associated with those changes.

Lesson 2

Students review Lesson 1, completing a Concept Review sheet to demonstrate what they have learned. The teacher models exhaustive scientific observation, and students practice this type of descriptive analysis. Students' concept knowledge is reinforced by brainstorming and comparing lists of examples of physical and chemical changes in a game format.

Lesson 3

Students view a list of common food products and kitchen tools that will be used in Lesson 4. Students develop data collection tables that will enable them to complete the experiments. Students preview the experiments that they will conduct in Lesson 4, form hypotheses, form lab teams, and review the scientific method.

Lesson 4

First, the teacher reviews safety protocol. Using the materials from Lesson 3, students visit stations in the lab and perform as many experiments as possible. (Lab teams of three students each are suggested, although fewer students could also work. Alternatively, the teacher could conduct all of the experiments as demonstrations.) Students follow experiment protocol to determine the types of changes that occur. Teams complete their data collection tables. (*Note*: This lesson requires 3 days).

Lesson 5

Lab teams meet to organize their findings and to review the rubric that will be used to evaluate presentations. The rubric includes visual, oral, and content components. The teacher discusses visual aids and the elements of successful presentations. Students develop visual aids that will assist them in presenting their data. Presenters gather constructive criticism from their classmates and reflect on how to improve their presentation skills. (*Note*: This lesson requires 2 days).

Lesson 6

The concept of authentic performance assessment is introduced. The teacher distributes the prompt for the final project, in which lab teams develop their own experiments. The rubric for the final project is distributed and materials are assembled that students will use to develop their own experiments. (*Note*: This lesson requires 2 days).

Lesson 7

Students gather materials and set up the experiments they have designed in the lab. Each team conducts the experiments it designed, enabling team members to make adjustments as necessary. During the second and third days, lab teams complete as many peer experiments as possible, carefully following the given protocols and documenting observations. The information generated by experimenters will be redistributed to the experiment designers in Lesson 8, enabling the creators of the experiments to reflect on their work and make presentations. (*Note*: This lesson requires 3 days).

Lesson 8

The rubric for the final project is revisited. Lab teams gather feedback on the experiments they have designed. Students create visual aids and organize their data into a presentation of their findings. Some students may prefer to use the computer lab to develop visual aids. Presentations are delivered and assessed using the final rubric and self-reflection materials. (*Note*: This lesson requires 2 days).

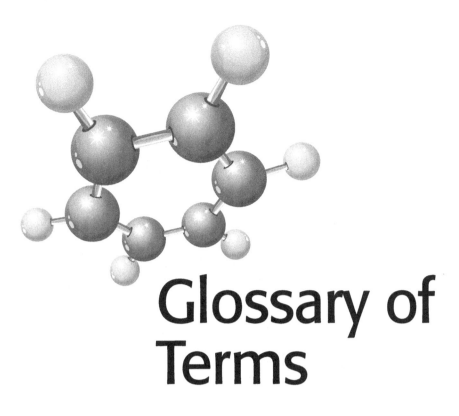

Glossary of Terms

For the purposes of this unit, the following definitions will be used.

- **Chemical Change:** A change that occurs that irreversibly changes matter into a different form; such a change is caused by the absorption or loss of energy.
- **Conclusion:** A decision, judgment, or opinion reached by reasoning.
- **Experiment:** A trial or test to explore an unknown or to verify a hypothesis.
- **Hypothesis:** A proposed explanation or prediction that seems logical or likely to be true; it is tested by experimentation.
- **Inference:** Using one's experience and what one has measured to reason about what something is or how something happens.
- **Physical Change:** A change that does not alter matter and is usually reversible.
- **Prediction:** A forecast of what will happen in the future; prediction is based on experience and observation.
- **Qualitative Observation:** The act of using sight, smell, touch, hearing, and taste to describe an object or a situation.
- **Quantitative Observation:** Using numbers and empirical, objective data to describe an object or situation.

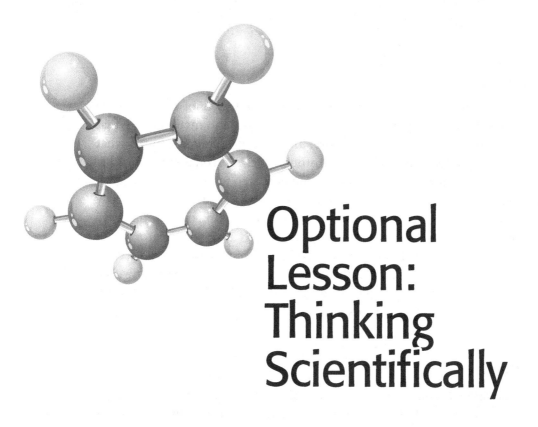

Optional Lesson: Thinking Scientifically

Concepts

- Qualitative observation
- Quantitative observation
- Organization/classification
- Inference
- Predicting

Materials

- Qualitative Observation sheet (p. 21)
- Quantitative Observation sheet (p. 22)
- Steepness of a Roof sheet (pp. 23–24)
- Prediction sheet (pp. 25–26)
- Final Paragraph sheet (p. 27)

Student Objective

The student will become familiar with the rigor of scientific thinking by completing the materials provided to sharpen the skills of observation, classifying data in an organized manner, drawing inferences, and making predictions.

Introduction

Thinking scientifically is an acquired skill. Few middle-school students have had the opportunity to be exposed to the underlying rigor and methodology that leads to making predictions about the future. They simply take for granted what they see, informally filter that information through their personal screens of life experiences, and judge (or more often, guess) the next step to be taken in order to solve a problem. We have chosen to make this lesson optional, being that you may be leading a class that has already been taught scientific thinking or that may have been presented with such an opportunity in an extracurricular setting. If many of your students have had access to museums, trips, and summer camps or have been surrounded by books from an early age, this lesson may be unnecessary. If, however, you have found that your students lack the ability to make or verbalize detailed observations, then this lesson may be useful.

Recognition

The teacher models qualitative observation skills by choosing an object in the classroom (unspecified to students) and generating an exhaustive list of its attributes. This may include, but should not to be limited to, color, texture, the sound that the object makes when dropped, and any odor the object may emit. This process continues until the students are able to correctly identify the object. This process may be repeated so that students understand the value of detailed observations. The teacher then proceeds to demonstrate quantitative observation skills by determining the length, width, height, mass, and density of the object, delving further into the definitions and associated equations of these as necessary.

Application

Students use the materials provided to sharpen their powers of observation.
1. Students complete the Qualitative Observation sheet, wherein they describe objects qualitatively and see if their classmates can guess what these objects are.
2. Students complete the Quantitative Observation sheet, wherein they measure objects selected by the teacher and record the objects' length, mass, density, and so forth.

Problem Solving

Students use the concepts they have learned to consider a real-world issue.
1. Using the Steepness of a Roof sheet as a guide, students make qualitative and quantitative observations of the roofs in the community and draw infer-

ences explaining why the roofs are relatively steep or flat. This sheet is completed for homework. In class the following day, a discussion is conducted about Question #3 on the sheet so that students learn to draw inferences from their observations.

2. Students complete the Prediction sheet, working in groups of three.
3. Students complete the Final Paragraph sheet.

Additional Notes

- On Day 1 of this lesson, be sure to have measuring tools (e.g., rulers, yardsticks, meter sticks, tape measures, balances) available for students to use while completing the Quantitative Observation sheet using random objects that you have selected.
- At the end of Day 1, have students organize the observations they have made by subject area. For example, in which class(es) would they be most likely to discuss the texture of objects, the color of objects, the density of materials, and the other attributes that have been listed on their worksheets? Point out that organizing and classifying data helps us to recall and understand information.
- As you assign the Steepness of a Roof sheet, remind students that pitch is defined as rise over run. This is also the definition of "slope" that they have studied or will study in their math classes. This is a great opportunity for you to collaborate with the math teacher on your team, should you wish to expand on this activity.
- Also, as you assign the Steepness of a Roof sheet, discuss the instructions with students. Some students may live in homes that do not allow them to complete this activity (e.g., high rises, condominiums). In this case, suggest that students find other buildings for which they can conduct the activity (e.g., a church, a restaurant). You could also direct them to research a gabled roof online, such as that of the Muchalls Castle.
- As you lead the discussion of the Steepness of a Roof sheet on Day 2, you may want to make students aware that in the northern part of the country, roofs are generally steeper in order to minimize the effects of greater downward force (snow load), whereas in southern locations, pitches are relatively flatter in order to minimize greater horizontal force (wind load). Students should understand that careful consideration of their observations will lead them to draw inferences. Further, they should understand that considering observations and inferences will enable them to make predictions (see the Prediction sheet for specific examples).
- We suggest that students work in groups of three when completing the Prediction sheet. This task can be quite a challenge, as students may have very different life experiences. It is also possible that students may not have

had a particular experience (e.g., paddling a kayak) that will enable them to make predictions. This will provide you with the opportunity to introduce the concept of conjecture, which allows us to make predictions of future events using the experiences of others.

- With respect to the Final Paragraph sheet, among the conclusions that students might reach are that scientific thinkers can be found in many walks of life, that they must be able to observe the world around them, and that they must be curious about what they see, smell, taste, hear, and touch. Such curiosity leads to asking why things are the way they are. Scientific thinkers organize their observations and inferences to make predictions about future events and must be creative in finding innovative solutions to problems.

Qualitative Observation

Do you remember what you saw yesterday on your way home from school? Did you get home without paying attention to what was going on around you? Scientists must train themselves to observe, notice, and record events that they witness every day.

Take a careful look at an item of clothing that someone in your class is wearing. List at least 10 attributes associated with the item of clothing you have chosen—for example, its color.

1. _____
2. _____
3. _____
4. _____
5. _____
6. _____
7. _____
8. _____
9. _____
10. _____

Using only the attributes that you have listed, write a paragraph describing the item of clothing you selected, then pass it on to a classmate designated by your teacher. Can your classmate identify the item after having read your paragraph? Explain what made it particularly easy or difficult for your classmate to use your observations to identify the item.

_____

_____

_____

_____

_____

_____

_____

Quantitative Observation

Select an item from those provided by your teacher and describe it using specific measurements and data. Be sure to include the proper units that you are using when taking measurements.

---

1. Object:

a. Length: b. Mass:

c. Width: d. Volume:

e. Height: f. Density:

---

2. Object:

a. Length: b. Mass:

c. Width: d. Volume:

e. Height: f. Density:

---

3. Object:

a. Length: b. Mass:

c. Width: d. Volume:

e. Height: f. Density:

---

4. Object:

a. Length: b. Mass:

c. Width: d. Volume:

e. Height: f. Density:

---

5. Object:

a. Length: b. Mass:

c. Width: d. Volume:

e. Height: f. Density:

---

6. Object:

a. Length: b. Mass:

c. Width: d. Volume:

e. Height: f. Density:

Understanding Physical and Chemical Changes © Prufrock Press Inc.

Steepness of a Roof

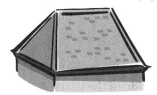

Use this sheet to guide you as you observe some attributes, take some measurements, and draw some inferences about the roof of the house in which you live or another nearby building.

1. List 10 attributes of the roof (such as color):

   a. _____

   b. _____

   c. _____

   d. _____

   e. _____

   f. _____

   g. _____

   h. _____

   i. _____

   j. _____

2. Use the directions below to determine the pitch, or steepness, of your roof. Remember that pitch is the change in vertical distance of the roof divided by the change in horizontal distance of the roof (rise over run).

   a. Determine the width of the house by taking a measurement. If a large measuring device is unavailable, you may simply "step it off," meaning that you can measure how many steps it takes to get from one end to the other, then measure the length of each step. What is the width of the house? (Note that this is a quantitative measurement.)

   _____

   b. Divide the result you found above in half to get the distance from one side of the house to the center. This is the horizontal distance change.

   _____

c. Approximate the change in the roof's vertical direction, or the height of the roof from the base (bottom) of the slope to the peak (top), by sighting or using some other means. Do **not** climb ladders or take any other measures that might put you in danger.

_____

d. Determine the pitch or slope of the roof by dividing the height (rise) of the roof by the width (run) of the roof from the side of the house to the center.

_____

3. In a few sentences, explain why you think the roof was designed with the particular pitch that you have found. Using what you know and have measured in order to explain something is called "inference."

_____

_____

_____

_____

_____

_____

_____

_____

_____

Name:_____ Date: _____

Prediction

Making predictions about what will happen in the future is based on the observations (qualitative and quantitative) you have made and by understanding why those observations matter and what they might mean (inference). Inference is based on your knowledge of the world around you. Predict what you would do if confronted with the following situations, and then explain why you would take those actions.

1. Situation: You come upon an angry, hissing cat with its claws extended. What would you do? (Prediction)

_____

_____

_____

Why? (Inference)

_____

_____

_____

2. Situation: You didn't have time to complete a major assignment. What will your teacher say? (Prediction)

_____

_____

_____

Why? (Inference)

_____

_____

_____

3. Situation: You are paddling along in a kayak and it begins to leak. What would you do? (Prediction)

_____

_____

_____

Why? (Inference)

_____

_____

_____

4. Situation: Someone you don't know sends you a friend request on Facebook. What would you do? (Prediction)

_____

_____

_____

Why? (Inference)

_____

_____

_____

5. Situation: You have attended an afterschool activity, and your ride was supposed to pick you up at 4:00 but still hasn't arrived at 4:30. What would you do? (Prediction)

_____

_____

_____

Why? (Inference)

_____

_____

_____

Final Paragraph

You have learned that when you make qualitative and quantitative observations and answer the question of why something is the way it is, why something happens the way it does, and so on, you are able to make inferences about an object or a situation. As you carefully consider observations and inferences and answer *What?* questions, you are able to make predictions.

Write a paragraph describing a person who thinks scientifically. Be sure to include how such a person would behave, the type of job he or she might hold, the qualities you would expect this person to have, and any other attributes you can think of.

_____

_____

_____

_____

_____

_____

_____

_____

_____

_____

_____

_____

_____

_____

_____

_____

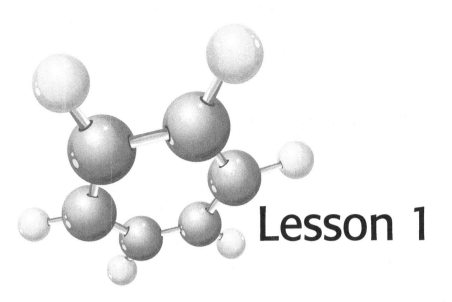

Lesson 1

Concepts

- Physical change
- Chemical change
- Irreversibility

Materials

- Concept posters (pp. 31–36)
- Menu of Demonstration Examples sheet (pp. 37)

Student Objective

Students demonstrate any knowledge they already have of physical and chemical changes.

Introduction

The teacher uses the concept posters provided that define physical and chemical changes. Several examples are included.

Recognition

Students complete a Type 1 John Collins writing piece. Using a blank sheet of paper, students write down everything they know about physical changes. Turning the paper over, they write down everything they know about chemical changes.

Application

The teacher demonstrates examples of physical and chemical changes and checks for understanding, repeating as necessary.

1. The teacher demonstrates an example of physical change, using the list of suggested examples on page 37 or another that he or she prefers, and asks what type of change it is. The teacher can have students respond individually (e.g., write down the answer on an understanding check, flash a "Physical Change" card or a "Chemical Change" card), or call on a student. Students should justify their decisions with reasons, and any misunderstandings should be clarified.

2. This process should be repeated with an example of a chemical change, and the teacher should offer additional examples and discuss explanations if necessary.

Problem Solving

The teacher has a conversation with students that deepens students' understanding of physical and chemical changes.

1. The teacher uses open-ended questions to initiate an exploration by students of the concepts of physical and chemical change (e.g., "Why do you suppose we study physical and chemical changes?" "What do you suppose actually happens when a match is struck?" "What do you suppose happens when I color a piece of paper red?").

2. Students hypothesize and discuss what all chemical changes and physical changes have in common. The teacher should guide students to understand that in chemical changes, energy is either absorbed or released through a chemical reaction, whereas in physical changes, matter undergoes a change in shape, size, or phase.

Additional Notes

- The posters and handouts included can be used in a variety of ways. You might use them to make your own PowerPoint, or you could show them to the class using a document camera. You could also make copies for students to have, or you could post the materials around the room so that students will be reminded of the concepts throughout the unit.

- Students should be made aware that the writing exercise will not be used for a grade. It is simply a tool with which to determine their level of prior knowledge. You may decide to collect their free writes, possibly incorporating them into the problem-solving discussion, or you may tell students to keep their definitions and amend them as they learn more.

- In our experience, students need a fairly thorough discussion of physical and chemical change in order to understand the concept of energy conservation and release. Thus, even after reviewing the concept posters with them, the questioning activity and discussion is very important, and further review will likely be necessary in the next few lessons.

- When discussing indicators of physical and chemical changes, you might tie the concepts back to the optional lesson and the discussion of inference. A student might use inference or reasoning with past knowledge and experience to say that an odor is an indication of a chemical change—the example of an egg cooking, for instance. However, odor is also given off when an onion is diced, which is a physical change. Likewise, coloring a piece of paper red is a physical change, because no energy is absorbed or lost, but cooking an egg (a chemical change) changes its color from translucent to white. Students may need to discuss the concept that indicators are not concrete proof of either a physical or chemical change having occurred.

There are two types of changes in the natural world . . .

Physical Changes

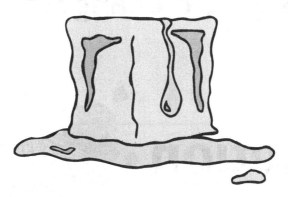

and

Chemical Changes

Physical Change
A physical change in a substance doesn't change what that substance is. Often, a physical change can be reversed.

Forces That Can Cause Physical Changes

Motion

Temperature

Pressure

Understanding Physical and Chemical Changes © Prufrock Press Inc.

Indicators of Physical Changes

Weight

Size

Density
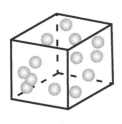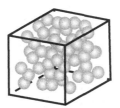

Texture

Shape

Volume

Chemical Changes
A chemical change alters matter irreversibly so that it is changed into something entirely different through lost or absorbed energy.

Absorbs Energy

Loses Energy

Understanding Physical and Chemical Changes © Prufrock Press Inc.
Permission is granted to photocopy or reproduce this page for single classroom use only.

Indicators of Chemical Changes

Change in Form and/or Color

Emitting Light, Heat, or Sound

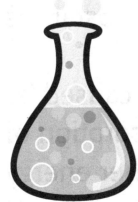

Forming Gases (Bubbles)

Physical vs. Chemical Changes

Physical Changes

Can often be reversed

Are often caused by motion, force, or temperature

Size, shape, or phase are changed

Chemical Changes

Are irreversible and turn substances into different substances

Are often caused by a loss or absorption of heat or other energy

Menu of Demonstration Examples

Physical Changes

- Demonstrator tears a piece of paper in half.
- Demonstrator colors a piece of paper with a crayon.
- Demonstrator crushes a can or a sheet of aluminum foil as tightly as possible.
- Demonstrator cuts off a small piece of his or her own hair.
- Demonstrator boils water.
- Demonstrator melts an ice cube.

Chemical Changes

- Demonstrator eats a small candy or sips some water and then moves around the room, simulating a transformation of fuel to energy.
- Demonstrator places 1 oz of HCl in a 50-mL beaker and tests the substance with litmus paper to determine acidity. The demonstrator cuts up a disposable aluminum pie plate and puts the pieces into the beaker. There will be a smoky reaction. Once this has subsided, the demonstrator should again use the litmus test. Once neutrality has been reached, the demonstrator may eat a small amount of the salt-like aluminum chloride paste for dramatic effect (but should not allow students to do so).
- Demonstrator strikes an unlit match, lets it burn for a few seconds, and blows it out.
- Demonstrator burns a peanut or other food or lights a candle.

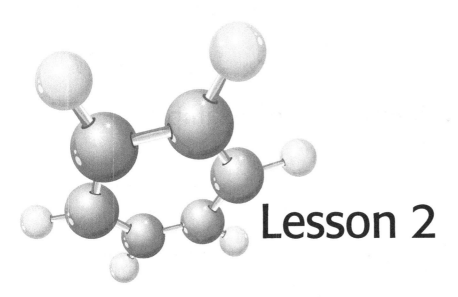

Lesson 2

Concepts
- Physical change
- Chemical change

Materials
- Concept Review sheet (pp. 41–42)

Student Objective

Students reinforce their understanding of physical and chemical changes by brainstorming lists in a game format.

Introduction

The teacher reviews the definitions of physical and chemical changes by referring to the concept posters from the previous lesson, and the students complete the Concept Review sheet to ensure that they understand the concepts from Lesson 1. The teacher models good observation techniques by describing in detail a process of change (e.g., "As the vinegar is added to the baking soda, bubbles begin to form . . .").

Recognition

Students look out a window and describe in detail the first object they see. They do this on paper, listing as many attributes of the object as possible (e.g., color, texture, size, distance away). They may work in pairs or individually.

Application

Students work in pairs to review their knowledge of physical and chemical changes.

1. Students either choose or are assigned partners. (If they completed the Recognition section in pairs, they may simply stay with their previous partners.)
2. Each pair of students writes down as many examples as possible of physical and chemical changes within a given time frame (set by the teacher). They should write physical changes on one side of the paper and chemical changes on the other side.
3. Once time is called, the groups share how many changes they have come up with. The teacher selects the pair with the most changes listed (either separately for the physical and chemical lists, or for the combined number of changes), and that pair reads its list(s) aloud.
4. The teacher verifies that each item is indeed a physical or chemical change, as listed. If other groups have the same items (correctly) on their lists as the items being read, they cross them off of their lists so that they won't read them, although they still count.
5. If the items on the first team's list are incorrect, the team with the next-highest number of items reads its list, and so forth. The team with the highest number of correct items wins.

Problem Solving

Students demonstrate that they remember the indicators of physical and chemical changes.

1. Each student writes a paragraph that describes the indicators of each type of change.
2. Students give examples in the paragraph showing how these indicators are seen in physical and chemical changes.
3. Encourage students to come up with examples not yet discussed in order to demonstrate their inference and reasoning abilities.
4. As an extra challenge, students can show how the same indicator (e.g., color, odor) can be representative of either a chemical or a physical change.

Additional Notes

- You can implement the Concept Review sheet in various ways. You could distribute the worksheet and then collect it, checking for individual understanding, you could do the exercise as a class, or you might have students work in pairs to discuss the concepts.

- Students often take for granted the attributes of objects they see every day. Encourage them to be specific and exhaustive in their assigned listing (description) of the object chosen in the Recognition section. We have had success having students select their own objects (either out the window or in the classroom), but you could also assign objects or have a random drawing.

- You may model a description you create yourself, if you like, and perhaps incorporate a review discussion of both qualitative and quantitative factors. We have learned that having a prepared script of a detailed description of a classroom object and sharing it with students is helpful. This guided practice gives students an actual example they can follow.

- It is up to you how to treat the Recognition exercise—you might collect students' writing exercises and remark on their level of detail, you might have students switch papers and give one another constructive criticism (and guess each other's objects), or you may simply use the exercise as a way of getting students into the scientific mindset.

- Once students complete the Problem Solving section, you can collect their written paragraphs and check for understanding. Although they list indicators of physical and chemical changes in the Concept Review sheet, this exercise will give you a better idea of which students need help with reasoning, inference, and drawing conclusions.

- In practice, we have learned that providing detailed descriptions while collecting data is a weakness for most students. Please take time to help students increase their powers of observation and to develop the language they use to describe objects and events. Honing this ability will increase their success as they apply the scientific method to perform the upcoming experiments.

Lesson 2

Name:_____ Date: _____

Concept Review

Physical vs. Chemical Change

1. A physical change is:

    _____

    _____

    _____

    _____

2. Circle the correct responses:

    A physical change **does/does not** change what the substance is.

    A physical change **can/cannot** be reversed.

3. Draw and label three examples of physical changes.

    _____ _____ _____

4. What are some indicators of physical change?

    _____

    _____

    _____

    _____

5. A chemical change is:

    _____

    _____

    _____

    _____

6. Circle the correct responses:

    A chemical change **does**/**does not** change what the substance is.

    A chemical change **can**/**cannot** be reversed.

7. Draw and label three examples of chemical changes.

    ┌──────────────┐ ┌──────────────┐ ┌──────────────┐
    │   │ │   │ │   │
    │   │ │   │ │   │
    │   │ │   │ │   │
    │   │ │   │ │   │
    │   │ │   │ │   │
    │   │ │   │ │   │
    └──────────────┘ └──────────────┘ └──────────────┘
    _____   _____   _____

8. What are some indicators of chemical change?

    _____

    _____

    _____

    _____

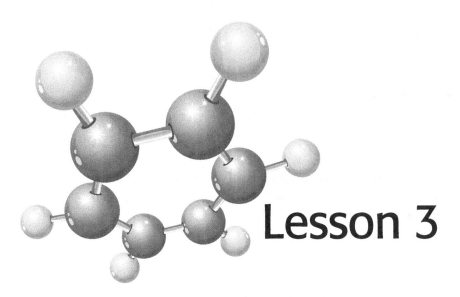

Lesson 3

Concepts

- Physical change
- Chemical change
- Scientific method

Materials

- Materials List sheet (pp. 46–47)
- Data Collection sheet (student version; p. 48)
- Data Collection sheet (teacher version; pp. 49–50)
- Experiment Overview sheet (p. 51)

Student Objective

Students show an understanding of the scientific method by organizing their information and forming hypotheses prior to conducting experiments in Lesson 4.

Introduction

The teacher distributes the Materials List sheet and leads a discussion of the food products on it, mentioning that all of the materials are fairly common and easy to find, discussing any safety precautions to be exercised, introducing any desired extension concepts (e.g., fats, carbohydrates, proteins), and offering brief explanations of each experiment to be conducted (e.g., "In Experiment #1, we will be applying lemon juice to an apple"). To preview the experiments, the teacher can either distribute the provided Experiment Overview sheet or simply describe the experiments verbally as students take notes. The teacher also discusses the purpose of the

Data Collection sheet, paying particular attention to the role that careful observations play in completing such a sheet.

Recognition

Students participate in a discussion of the importance of observation, forming a hypothesis, and conducting experimentation prior to drawing conclusions. This can be a whole-class discussion or a small-group discussion.

Application

Students brainstorm about how they will use inference and hypotheses to assist in their experimentation.

1. Students form lab teams of no more than three students per team.
2. Working in teams, students discuss questions that will need to be answered in order to decide whether a physical or chemical change has occurred.

Problem Solving

Students work collaboratively to prepare for the experiments in the next lesson.

1. Working in their lab teams, students complete all parts of the Data Collection sheet that they can.
2. Students hypothesize about what will happen in the various experiments, using inference and reasoning.

Additional Notes

- We have not provided any explicit review of the scientific method, given its prevalence in science textbooks, but you may discuss or review the process with the students to whatever degree is necessary depending on their previous experience. This may be a good time to step outside of the unit and provide some direct instruction.
- The Data Collection sheet is comprised of four columns, the first two of which are self-explanatory. In the "Type of Change" column, students should list their predictions as to what type of change they think will occur for a given experiment. In the "Indicators" column, students should elaborate on the questions that will need to be addressed in order to move from their observations to the final conclusions they reach. Essentially, students are making a map of the thinking and reasoning they will be doing when they conduct the experiments and record their results in Lesson 4. They are also hypothesizing about what the experiments' results will be based upon what

they have learned thus far (and what they already know about the experiments' components).

- Students will tend to jump to conclusions rather than being methodical in their approach as they complete their Data Collection sheets. Remind them of how completely they listed the attributes of objects in Lesson 2. Coach them to continue to be exhaustive in their observations as they review the Materials List sheet and the Data Collection sheet in this lesson.
- Some of the materials listed may not be appropriate for your classroom (e.g., students must not bring knives or foods to which other students are allergic). After previewing the experiments, you may make modifications to the experiments provided, or you may substitute your own experiment(s).

Materials List

Experiment 1: An Apple a Day

- Apple
- Knife
- Lemon juice
- Two paper cups
- Tablespoon measure
- Small container with lid
- Pen or marker

Experiment 2: Anchors Away

- Plastic soda bottle (liter)
- One large balloon (18 inches)
- One teaspoon baking soda
- Three tablespoons vinegar
- Scotch tape
- Measuring spoons
- Funnel

Experiment 3: How Do You Like Your Toast?

- Toaster
- Two slices of bread
- Paper plates
- Knife

Experiment 4: Egg Shell

- One uncooked egg
- One cup of vinegar
- Clear containers large enough to hold egg and vinegar
- Labels
- Permanent marker

Experiment 5: Soda or Powder?

- Water bottle
- Baking powder
- Baking soda
- Two beakers or clear cups
- Masking tape
- Permanent marker

Understanding Physical and Chemical Changes © Prufrock Press Inc.

Experiment 6: Milkshake, Anyone?

- ❑ Water
- ❑ Whole milk
- ❑ Two beakers (100 mL)
- ❑ Eyedroppers
- ❑ Vinegar
- ❑ Small bucket

Experiment 7: Marshmallow Roast

- ❑ Mini marshmallows
- ❑ Foil cupcake liners
- ❑ Hot plate
- ❑ Paper and pen
- ❑ Plastic spoons

Experiment 8: Plop, Plop, Fizz, Fizz

- ❑ Two 8-oz clear cups
- ❑ Water
- ❑ Salt
- ❑ Alka Seltzer tablets
- ❑ Straws
- ❑ Masking tape
- ❑ Permanent marker
- ❑ Tablespoon measure

Experiment 9: Chocolate Heaven

- ❑ Chocolate bars
- ❑ Foil cupcake liners
- ❑ Hot plate
- ❑ Spoons
- ❑ Paper and pen

Experiment 10: Rainbow

- ❑ Food coloring
- ❑ Water
- ❑ Clear cups (6–8 oz)
- ❑ Paper and pen
- ❑ Marker

Name:_____ Date: _____

Data Collection

Use the back of this sheet or additional paper as necessary.

Experiment Number and Title	Description of Materials	Type of Change	Indicators

Understanding Physical and Chemical Changes © Prufrock Press Inc.

Data Collection Answer Key

Experiment Number and Title	Description of Materials	Type of Change	Indicators
1. An Apple a Day	Apple, knife, lemon juice, two paper cups, tablespoon measure, small container with lid	Chemical	The enzymes in the apple react to the oxygen in the air and begin to digest the cells of the apple, causing discoloration and a change in taste. The citric acid in the lemon juice prevents this occurrence by reacting with the enzyme before the oxidation process can begin.
2. Anchors Away	Plastic soda bottle (liter), one large balloon (18 inches), one teaspoon baking soda, three tablespoons vinegar, scotch tape, measuring spoons	Chemical	A chemical reaction occurs when the vinegar and baking soda are mixed, releasing carbon dioxide. The carbon dioxide fills the balloon.
3. How Do You Like Your Toast?	Toaster, two slices of bread, paper plates, knife	Both	Physical: When the bread is lightly toasted, the color and temperature changes, but not the molecular structure. Chemical: Burned spots of toast show a chemical change, because the bread has actually been changed into a burnt, ash-like substance.
4. Egg Shell	One uncooked egg, one cup of vinegar, clear containers large enough to hold egg and vinegar, labels, permanent marker	Chemical	The vinegar dissolves the eggshell (made of calcium carbonate) into calcium and carbon dioxide.
5. Soda or Powder?	Water bottle, baking powder, baking soda, two beakers or clear cups, masking tape, permanent marker	Chemical	The acid in baking powder reacts with the water to produce carbon dioxide, which is evident when bubbles are produced. This occurs with baking soda as well, but to a lesser degree.

Data Collection Answer Key, continued

Experiment Number and Title	Description of Materials	Type of Change	Indicators
6. Milkshake, Anyone?	Water, whole milk, two beakers (100 mL), eyedroppers, vinegar in beakers, small bucket	Chemical	The acid in the vinegar reacts with the lactose in the milk to transform it into milk solids. This does not occur with the vinegar and water, which undergoes no chemical change.
7. Marshmallow Roast	Mini marshmallows, foil cupcake liners, hot plate, paper, pen, plastic spoons	Both	Physical: When the marshmallow is torn in half, it is a physical change caused by force. Chemical: When the marshmallow is heated to the point of burning, a chemical change occurs, changing the marshmallow into a different substance. Prior to burning (when the marshmallow is only melted), a physical change has occurred.
8. Plop, Plop, Fizz, Fizz	Two 8-oz clear cups, water, salt, Alka Seltzer tablets, straws, masking tape, permanent marker, tablespoon measure	Both	Physical: When the salt is added to the water, it changes the taste but does not change the molecular structure. Chemical: The Alka Seltzer tablet reacts with the water to produce bubbles of carbon dioxide.
9. Chocolate Heaven	Chocolate bars, foil cupcake liners, hot plate, spoons, paper, pen	Both	Melted chocolate changes with regard to form and texture, but remains the same substance—until it is burned, at which point it changes into a different substance.
10. Rainbow	Food coloring, water, clear cups (6–8 oz), paper, pen	Physical	Food coloring changes the color of the water, but not the water itself. As more water is added, the color fades.

Experiment Overview

More information and instructions are provided in Lesson 4.

1. **An Apple a Day.** Students will cut apple pieces and will cover some of them with lemon juice. They will leave the apple pieces out in the open and will observe what happens to them.

2. **Anchors Away.** Students will mix baking soda and vinegar in a bottle, attach a balloon to the mouth of the bottle, and observe the results.

3. **How Do You Like Your Toast?** Students will toast slices of bread and will observe what happens to the bread as the toaster is put on different settings (e.g., light, dark).

4. **Egg Shell.** Students will place an egg in a clear container full of vinegar and will observe what happens after 24 hours.

5. **Soda of Powder?** Students will add water to both baking powder and baking soda and observe what occurs.

6. **Milkshake, Anyone?** Students will add vinegar to both water and milk and observe what occurs.

7. **Marshmallow Roast.** Students will heat marshmallows to various degrees and will observe what changes occur.

8. **Plop, Plop, Fizz, Fizz.** Students will add both salt and Alka Seltzer to cups of water and will observe the results.

9. **Chocolate Heaven.** Students heat chocolate to various degrees and observe the results.

10. **Rainbow.** Students will begin with cups of water and will add food coloring, then additional various quantities of water, observing the results.

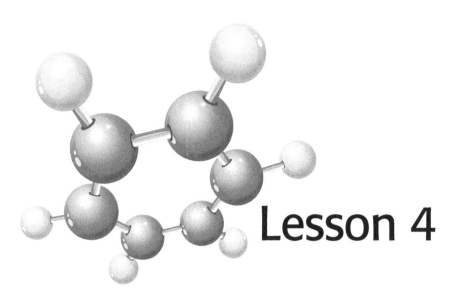

Lesson 4

Concepts

- Physical change
- Chemical change
- Scientific method

Materials

- Experiment posters (pp. 54–63)
- Process Observation sheet (p. 64)
- Data Collection sheets (p. 48; one per student)
- Materials for experiments

Student Objective

Students conduct 10 experiments. Observations are made and recorded over a 3-day period. Students compile data and make inferences about the nature of the changes they have observed.

Introduction

The teacher reviews the safety protocol to be followed while performing experiments. (This safety review is repeated daily.) The teacher emphasizes the importance of recording accurate and descriptive observations.

Recognition

Students review the instruction sheet for each experiment. Teachers can either photocopy the experiment posters provided and make packets, or display each poster in front of the corresponding experiment and have students circulate around the room to preview the experiments, asking any questions they may have.

Application

Students conduct the experiments.
1. Students should understand which experiments require more than a single class period.
2. Students conduct the experiments in lab teams of three.
3. Students record observations on individual Data Collection sheets.

Problem Solving

Students collaborate with their lab teams to draw conclusions.
1. Once students have completed all of the experiments, they will discuss their results in their lab teams.
2. Students will compare the data they have collected from the experiments and will complete the final lab team version of the Data Collection sheet.

Additional Notes

There are some options available to you:
- You have a few different options when it comes to running these experiments in your classroom. You could set up all 10 experiments in a lab station format such that students will visit each station over the span of 3 days (or more or fewer as you deem appropriate). Alternatively, you could set up three experiments on Day 1 of this lesson, three experiments on Day 2, and four experiments on Day 3.
- If time is an issue, you could also conduct each of the experiments yourself and simply have students observe the results. This may also be helpful if you have limited supplies, if some of your students should not be eating certain ingredients included in the materials, and so forth. If you decide to do this, have students make specific, exhaustive written observations of your processes. This is not our preferred method, as in our experience, most students learn best while actively engaged, but sometimes it makes the most sense.

Experiment 1: An Apple a Day

Materials

- ❑ Apple
- ❑ Knife
- ❑ Lemon juice
- ❑ Two paper cups

- ❑ Tablespoon measure
- ❑ Small container with lid
- ❑ Pen or marker

Procedure

1. Label one cup "Plain" and the other cup "Lemon Juice."
2. Label both cups with the names of your lab team members.
3. Cut the unpeeled apple into quarters.
4. Place one quarter in the paper cup labeled "Plain." Leave as much of the apple flesh exposed as possible (place the apple so that the side with the skin is down).
5. Place the second quarter (in the same position) in the paper cup marked "Lemon Juice."
6. Pour a tablespoon of lemon juice over the top of this quarter, doing your best to coat the entire exposed surface area of the apple (the flesh).
7. Allow both sections to remain uncovered as long as possible (overnight is recommended).
8. Observe and record the color and texture of each section.
9. Clean up the lab station.

Understanding Physical and Chemical Changes © Prufrock Press Inc.

Experiment 2: Anchors Away

Materials

- ❏ Plastic soda bottle (liter)
- ❏ One large balloon (18 inches)
- ❏ One teaspoon baking soda
- ❏ Three tablespoons vinegar
- ❏ Scotch tape
- ❏ Measuring spoons
- ❏ Funnel

Procedure

1. Pour 1 teaspoon of baking soda into the bottle.
2. Pour 3 tablespoons of vinegar into the balloon.
3. Attach the open end of the balloon to the mouth of the bottle, using tape to keep it in place. Be careful not to allow any vinegar to spill into the bottle!
4. Once the balloon is securely in place, raise the balloon and allow the vinegar to flow into the sealed bottle.
5. Record your observations.
6. Clean up the lab station.

Experiment 3: How Do You Like Your Toast?

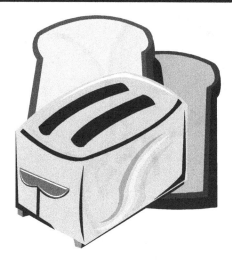

Materials

- ☐ Toaster
- ☐ Two slices of bread
- ☐ Paper plates
- ☐ Knife

Procedure

1. Cut both slices of bread in half.
2. Label four paper plates: "Untoasted," "Light," "Medium," and "Dark."
3. Set the toaster to the "Light" setting and begin toasting one half of a slice. Put the piece of bread in lengthwise so you can remove it easily once it is done.
4. Examine the untoasted slice of bread. Make observations about the aroma, texture, and appearance of the untoasted bread. Place it on the paper plate labeled "Untoasted," and record all of your observations.
5. When the lightly toasted piece of bread pops up, remove it carefully and observe it, recording any changes to its aroma, texture, appearance, and so forth. Place it on the paper plate labeled "Light."
6. Repeat this process with the toaster set to "Medium." Record your observations.
7. Repeat this process with the toaster set to "Dark." Record your observations.
8. Clean up your lab station.

Understanding Physical and Chemical Changes © Prufrock Press Inc.

Experiment 4: Egg Shell

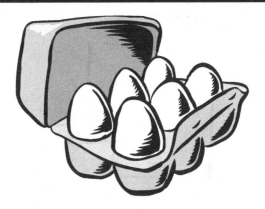

Materials

- ❑ One uncooked egg
- ❑ One cup of vinegar
- ❑ Clear containers large enough to hold egg and vinegar
- ❑ Labels
- ❑ Permanent marker

Procedure

1. Use a permanent marker and labels to label the container that your lab team will be using.
2. Carefully place an uncooked egg into this container. Be sure that you can see the egg through the container—do not block it with your label or anything else.
3. Pour 1 cup of vinegar into the container, making sure that the egg is submerged in the vinegar.
4. Seal the container and place it somewhere where it will not be disturbed.
5. Examine the egg after 24 hours and record your observations.

Experiment 5: Soda or Powder?

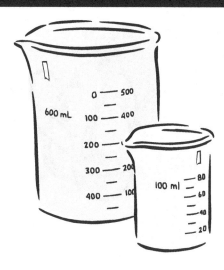

Materials

- ❑ Water bottle
- ❑ Baking powder
- ❑ Baking soda
- ❑ Two beakers or clear cups
- ❑ Masking tape
- ❑ Permanent marker

Procedure

1. Label one cup or beaker "Baking Soda."
2. Label one cup or beaker "Baking Powder."
3. Place 1 tablespoon of baking soda in the corresponding cup or beaker.
4. Place 1 tablespoon of baking powder in the corresponding cup or beaker.
5. Add 2 tablespoons of water to one of the cups or beakers. Record your observations.
6. Add 2 tablespoons of water to the other cup or beaker. Record your observations.
7. Clean up, throwing away the cups or washing the beakers.

Experiment 6: Milkshake, Anyone?

Materials

- ❑ Water
- ❑ Whole milk
- ❑ Two beakers (100 mL)
- ❑ Eyedroppers
- ❑ Vinegar
- ❑ Small bucket

Procedure

1. Label the beakers "Water" and "Milk."
2. Put 25 mL of water into the beaker labeled "Water."
3. Put 25 mL of milk into the beaker labeled "Milk."
4. Use the eyedropper to add three drops of vinegar to the water.
5. Allow this mixture to stand for 5–10 minutes. Record your observations.
6. Repeat with the other beaker, adding three drops of vinegar to the milk. Let stand for 5–10 minutes and record your observations.
7. Wash the beakers thoroughly.

Experiment 7: Marshmallow Roast

Materials

- ❏ Mini marshmallows
- ❏ Foil cupcake liners
- ❏ Hot plate
- ❏ Paper and pen
- ❏ Plastic spoons

Procedure

1. Label one piece of paper "Melted" and another piece of paper "Crusty."
2. Place two cupcake liners, each one holding three marshmallows, on the hot plate.
3. Stir the marshmallows so that they melt evenly. Use **extreme caution** when near the hot plate.
4. Tear a raw marshmallow in half. Record your observations. Eat the raw marshmallow. Carefully observe its taste and texture. Record your results. Only one marshmallow per student!
5. When the melting marshmallows become liquid, remove one of the cupcake liners and place it on the piece of paper labeled "Melted." Allow it to cool, and then record your observations.
6. When the marshmallows still on the hot plate become crusty and dark, remove the liner and place it on the piece of paper labeled "Crusty." Record your observations.
7. After both samples are cool enough, use plastic spoons to sample a small amount from each cupcake liner. Record your observations.

Experiment 8:
Plop, Plop, Fizz, Fizz

Materials

- ❑ Two 8-oz clear cups
- ❑ Water
- ❑ Salt
- ❑ Alka Seltzer tablets
- ❑ Straws
- ❑ Masking tape
- ❑ Permanent marker
- ❑ Tablespoon measure

Procedure

1. Label the cups "Salt" and "Alka Seltzer."
2. Add equal amounts of water to the two cups.
3. Taste and observe the water. (Use straws to avoid spreading germs.)
4. Add 1 tablespoon of salt to the corresponding cup and stir. Taste the water from this cup and record your observations.
5. Place an Alka Seltzer tablet into the corresponding cup. Record your observations. **Do not taste.**

Experiment 9: Chocolate Heaven

Materials

- ❑ Chocolate bars
- ❑ Foil cupcake liners
- ❑ Hot plate
- ❑ Spoons
- ❑ Paper and pen

Procedure

1. Label one sheet of paper "Melted" and another sheet of paper "Crusty."
2. Eat a small rectangle of chocolate. Carefully note the taste and texture. Record your observations. Only one small rectangle per student!
3. Place two cupcake liners, each containing a small rectangle of chocolate, onto the hot plate. Use **extreme caution** around the hot plate.
4. Stir the chocolate as it melts. Once the melting chocolate has become liquid, remove one of the liners and place it on the paper labeled "Melted." Wait for the chocolate to cool. Record your observations.
5. Once the chocolate still on the hot plate becomes crusty and dark, remove it and place it on the piece of paper labeled "Crusty." Record your observations.
6. After both samples are cool enough, sample a small piece of chocolate from each cupcake liner using a plastic spoon. Record your observations.

Experiment 10: Rainbow

Materials

- ❏ Food coloring
- ❏ Water
- ❏ Clear cups (6–8 oz)
- ❏ Paper and pen
- ❏ Marker

Procedure

1. Label the paper cups "A," "B," and "C."
2. Pour 2 tablespoons of water into each cup.
3. Add 3 drops of food coloring to each cup. Use the same color for all three cups. You will only use one color; put equal amounts (three drops) in each cup.
4. Record your observations.
5. Pour 1/4 cup of water into Cup A.
6. Pour 1/2 cup of water into Cup B.
7. Pour 1 cup of water into Cup C.
8. Record your observations.

Name:_____ Date:_____

Process Observation

Title of experiment:

_____

Materials used:

_____   _____

_____   _____

_____   _____

_____   _____

Step-by-step observations:

Step 1:_____

_____

Step 2:_____

_____

Step 3:_____

_____

Step 4:_____

_____

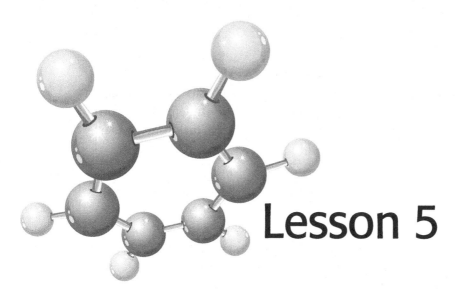

Lesson 5

Concepts

- Using visual aids to demonstrate findings
- Public speaking
- Enunciation
- Projection
- Eye contact

Materials

- Presentation Rubric sheet (p. 68)
- Concept posters (pp. 69–70)
- Materials for visual aids (e.g., poster paper, Microsoft Excel)

Student Objective

Working in their lab teams, students use the presentation rubric to develop lab team presentations in which they organize and present the data they collected in Lesson 4.

Introduction

The teacher reviews the need for data to be organized in order to enable conclusions to be drawn about the experiments. The teacher reviews the presentation rubric, offering examples and answering any questions students may have.

Recognition

Teams work to organize their data and use their observations to come to conclusions about the nature of the changes that were seen in the experiments. Students discuss the presentation rubric further in their groups. As a class, the students discuss the question to be answered by the data (e.g., whether a physical and/or chemical change occurred in each experiment). Also as a class, the students brainstorm visual aids that can be used to illustrate the groups' data and conclusions (e.g., chart, graph).

Application

Students share their teams' results by presenting to the class.
1. In their lab teams, students decide on what type of visual aid will be most helpful and appropriate for showing their results and data to the class.
2. Each team creates a visual aid to be used in its presentation.
3. Each team presents its findings to the class using the visual aid students have developed.
4. As students present, the teacher keeps track of each team's conclusions, displaying them on the board or in some other manner (i.e., shows each team's conclusions regarding whether changes were physical and/or chemical).
5. Depending on time constraints, students can offer teams constructive criticism on their presentations, either verbally or in writing. If this is included in the lesson, a conversation (including examples) about what constitutes constructive criticism may be useful prior to the start of the presentations.
6. Once all groups have presented, the class discusses and reflects on what the data represent (whether there is consensus or disagreement). If there is disagreement, the teacher guides the discussion, if necessary, to reach a consensus and understanding of what the various experiments indicated.

Problem Solving

Students evaluate their own presentations and visual aids.
1. Students reflect on their team's choice of visual aid, highlighting its strengths and weaknesses. If audience members offered verbal or written constructive criticism, this can be incorporated into the self-reflection.
2. Each team (or each individual student) writes a paragraph describing how the chosen visual aid and the data display could be improved.

Additional Notes

- You can break this lesson into parts depending on what works best for your schedule. We have found that it is most useful to devote the first day to preparation of the presentations, and the second day to the presentations and self-reflection.

- We suggest developing a master conclusion sheet and posting it either as an overhead projection or on the board. As each team presents its findings, post that team's conclusion about each experiment (physical and/or chemical change) on the master conclusion sheet. If a computer/LCD projector is available, these data could be entered into a spreadsheet, allowing the class to view the information in several formats (e.g., bar graph, T-chart). This master conclusion sheet also provides an easy and efficient way of checking for student understanding—and to facilitate grading, if you so choose.
- You may have students reflect on their team presentations either in groups or as individuals. Collect, review, and keep these written self-reflections, which will be returned to students in Lesson 8, as they are preparing their final presentations. (If they will stay in the same lab teams throughout the unit, then you may opt to have them complete the written self-reflection in teams, whereas if they will be changing groups, individual self-reflections may be less complicated.)

Presentation Rubric

	Sales CEO	Salesperson	Trainee
Visual Aid			
Appearance	The visual aid is eye-catching and communicates the information at first glance.	The visual aid is attractive and communicates the information after careful study.	The visual aid is hard to read and/or does not communicate any information.
Content	All of the information is accurate and essential.	All of the information is accurate, but some of it is not needed to make the point.	The information is not accurate.
Public Speaking			
Performance	The speakers are easy to hear and understand, and they regularly make eye contact with the audience.	The speakers can only sometimes be heard and/or understood, and eye contact is not consistent.	The speakers are difficult to hear and/or understand, and they make little to no eye contact.
Content	The spoken information is well organized.	The spoken information is accurate but hard to follow.	The spoken information is inaccurate and disorganized.

Visual Aids

What is a visual aid?

It's a graph, image, or other visual depiction of your data and ideas that boils things down for the audience.

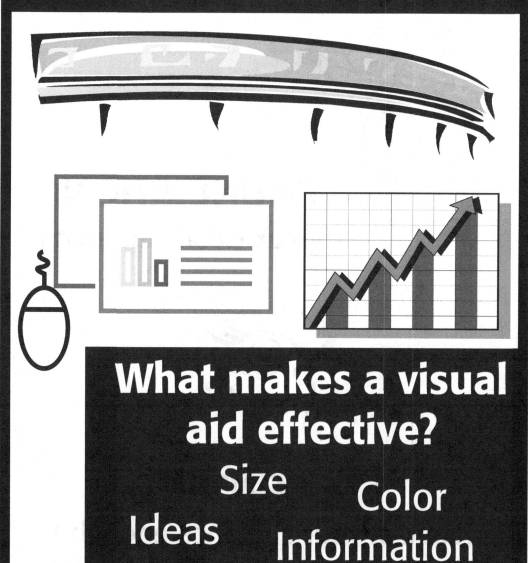

What makes a visual aid effective?

Size

Color

Ideas

Information

Public Speaking

PROJECTION
(Speak loudly enough.)

ENUNCIATION
(Speak clearly enough.)

EYE CONTACT
(Look at your audience enough.)

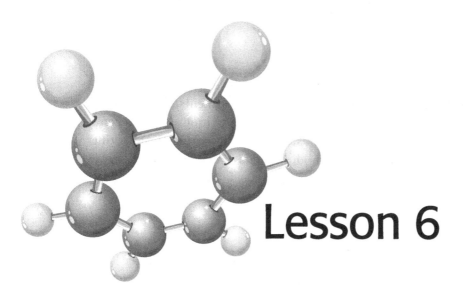

Lesson 6

Concepts

- Authentic performance assessment
- Using a rubric
- Designing an experiment

Materials

- Final Project Prompt sheet (p. 74)
- Final Project Rubric sheet (p. 75)
- Experimental Design sheets (pp. 76–77)
- Data Collection sheet (p. 78)

Student Objective

Students discuss the concept of an authentic performance assessment and receive the prompt for their final project. Students work to develop strategies to design original experiments.

Introduction

The teacher describes what an authentic performance assessment is and how it is used; the purpose of this discussion is for students to understand that they will be evaluated on their *application* of the concepts at hand, rather than merely on their understanding of those concepts. The teacher also reviews the elements of the scientific method, prompting the students to offer suggestions, examples, and explanations. With this discussion, students will be put into the scientific mindset.

Recognition

As the teacher is discussing authentic performance assessments, students contribute to the discussion with questions and examples (e.g., writing a song to demonstrate comprehension and application of music composition principles). During the teacher's discussion of the scientific method, students offer suggestions, examples, and explanations.

Application

Students receive the Final Project Prompt sheet, the Final Project Rubric sheet, the Experimental Design sheets, and the Data Collection sheet. (Note: It is left to the teacher to decide whether to have students work individually or in groups. If groups are selected, it is recommended that they be made up of three or fewer students.) Students read through the prompt individually or in small groups and list/discuss the tasks that must be accomplished to design an experiment.

Problem Solving

Students apply the concepts they have learned to design their own experiments.
1. Students use the Experiment Design sheets and the Data Collection sheet, being as thorough as possible.
2. When designing their experiments, students should keep in mind the concepts listed on the Final Project Rubric sheet.
3. Students must keep in mind and address each step in the scientific method.

Additional Notes

- Many students in traditional classrooms have little experience with authentic performance assessments—assessments that require them to apply what they have learned to create real-world projects, rather than simply reciting the concepts that have been reviewed. We find that it is helpful to discuss with students the merits of such authentic assessments—for example, increased creativity, increased confidence, room for innovation, opportunity for extension, and so forth. Some students who are used to traditional methods such as recitation and tests may need additional assurance that there are no right answers or set paths.
- We recommend having students work in teams of three or fewer. You may choose to allow students to continue working in the teams they've used previously, although this is a good time to make changes in lab team assignments if you have been having any issues. You may also decide to allow students to work individually, depending on what you've observed up until this point

Lesson 6

(and as time allows, given that this would require extra days for students to complete the experiments). Students are frequently more comfortable working in teams.

- Expect students to have difficulty with the task of designing an experiment. We have learned that trying to rush this step is not helpful. Coach students as needed, assuring them that the development of experiments is messy and there are no wrong answers or silly suggestions.

- You may break this lesson down into components as time allows. What has worked best for us has been to familiarize students with the final prompt, the final rubric, the design sheets, and the data collection table on the first day, and to devote the second day to having students actually complete the experimental protocol by listing step-by-step instructions that their classmates will use to perform the experiments.

- It is up to you how many points to assign for the categories included in the final project rubric. We have left it fairly open ended for grading purposes.

- Depending on your available resources and your class situation, you may opt to allow students to use external sources (e.g., the Internet) to prepare experiments. However, there are so many ready-made experiments available online that we often prefer to have students brainstorm and design their experiments the old-fashioned way, rooted in imagination and observation. It's always fun to see what students come up with for their own experiments—we have had students explore the workings of nail polish remover, experiment with how cereal can be transformed chemically and physically, and more!

- Depending on the availability of materials, time constraints, and the degree to which students are showing creativity, you may opt to have each lab team or individual student develop only one original experiment that demonstrates either a physical or a chemical change, as opposed to developing an experiment for each type of change.

Final Project Prompt

Igor Publishing

555 Main Street • City, State 55555 • Phone: (123) 456-7890

Congratulations! You and your colleagues have been hired by Igor Publishing, a textbook company, to develop a series of experiments for students that will be included in a new book entitled *Understanding Physical and Chemical Changes.*

Over the next several days, you must design two experiments: one showing a physical change, and the other showing a chemical change. You will complete a design packet for each experiment showing the experiment's components, procedure, and so forth.

Both of your experiments will be conducted by your peers according to the experimental design that you set forth. Your peers will test their hypotheses regarding your experiments, and they will also assess the quality of the experiments. We have provided a rubric to offer some guidance as you take on this challenge.

Once your experiments are set up so that your peers can conduct the experiments for themselves, you will write the title of each experiment on corresponding Data Collection sheets (however many are required) so that your peers can offer their feedback, hypotheses, and conclusions.

At the conclusion of the testing phase, your team will receive the data collected by your peers as they have conducted your experiments. You will use these data to develop a presentation on your findings, which you will present to your peers and the Research Director, your direct supervisor.

Should you have any questions regarding your assignment, the Research Director will be available to address your concerns. Your continued employment depends on your performance. Good luck!

Sincerely,

Edison Igor

Edison Igor, Publisher
Igor Publishing

Final Project Rubric

Igor Publishing
555 Main Street • City, State 55555 • Phone: (123) 456-7890

	Einstein	Scientist	Apprentice
Experimental Design	Your design was complete and easy to follow. All materials were provided and the protocol was accurate.	Your design was complete but was challenging to follow and/or not all of the materials were provided.	Your design was incomplete and hard to follow. Materials were not provided, making the experiment difficult to perform.
Findings and Conclusions	Your findings were well organized and presented clearly. Your conclusions were supported by your findings.	Your data were adequately presented but did not support your conclusions.	The data were incoherent and did not support your conclusions.
Visual Aid	Your visual aid was eye-catching and clearly represented your findings.	Your visual aid did not represent your conclusions or the findings were inaccurately displayed.	Your visual aid did not represent your findings, and the findings were inaccurate.
Presentation	You were clear and consistent in volume. Your body posture and delivery made it clear you were confident of the facts, lending believability to your presentation.	Your volume and pace were inconsistent, making it hard to follow your findings to their conclusion.	Your speech was difficult to hear due to poor volume and pace, making it hard to believe your findings. You lacked conviction.

Name:_____ Date: _____

Experimental Design

Complete the following, being as thorough as possible.

1. Experiment authors: _____

    _____

    _____

2. Question to be answered by experiment: _____

    _____

    _____

3. Hypothesis: _____

    _____

    _____

4. Materials needed (include where you will obtain materials from):

    _____   _____

    _____   _____

    _____   _____

    _____   _____

5. Potential safety issues (include how you will keep the experiment safe): _____

    _____

    _____

    _____

    _____

    _____

    _____

Understanding Physical and Chemical Changes © Prufrock Press Inc.

6. Experimental protocol (provide exact, step-by-step instructions, using additional paper as needed):

a. _____

_____

b. _____

_____

c. _____

_____

d. _____

_____

e. _____

_____

f. _____

_____

g. _____

_____

h. _____

_____

i. _____

_____

Data Collection

Experiment Name: _____

Name(s) of Experimenter(s)	Notes on Experimental Design	Hypothesis	Observations	Conclusion

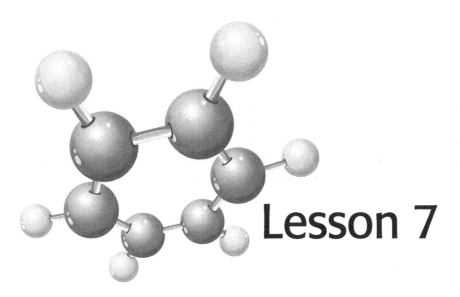

Lesson 7

Concepts

- Physical change
- Chemical change
- Scientific method

Materials

- Completed materials from Lesson 6 (including the appropriate number of Data Collection sheets)
- Self-Assessment sheet (p. 82)

Student Objective

Students set up the experiments they have designed. Their peers conduct the experiments and complete the Data Collection sheets.

Introduction

The teacher reviews safety protocol, clearing each experiment individually to ensure that it is safe, and reviews the steps and concepts necessary to complete an experiment successfully.

Recognition

Student lab teams present their experiments, materials, and safety protocols to the Research Director (teacher) for review and make any necessary modifications that he or she recommends.

Application

Students set up and run the experiments and offer feedback.

1. Students set up their experiments and test them for accuracy. Adjustments to protocol may be made at this time. The Self-Assessment sheet can be used to guide students as they review the instructions they have developed. This may bring to students' attention potential issues and instructions that require clarification.
2. Instructions for each experiment, whether explained on revised Experiment Design sheets or in another format, should be posted clearly.
3. Lab teams conduct one another's experiments as instructed in the Experiment Design sheets.

Problem Solving

Students complete the materials associated with the experiments.

1. Students read the instructions on the Experimental Design sheets for each experiment.
2. Students hypothesize, conduct experiments, make observations, and draw conclusions using the Data Collection sheets provided for each experiment.
3. Students should not comment on other teams' hypotheses or information, and neither should they be influenced by other teams' comments. (This can be avoided by having each team complete an entirely separate sheet.)
4. Data Collection sheets to be turned in to the Research Director for safe-keeping once they are completed.

Additional Notes

- We suggest the lab station approach, in which each lab team set up its experiment materials (after they are approved), along with the instructions the students have prepared. Each lab team then performs all of the experiments other than the ones they have designed. For example, if there are eight lab teams in the class, each with two experiments, then each team will complete 14 experiments—both of the experiments of the other seven teams.
- We like to have students make an eye-catching set of instructions for each experiment, although they may simply use revised Experimental Design sheets. It can be fun for artistic-minded students to design mini-posters with pictorial instructions for the experiments.
- Remind students that they are not permitted to ask the creators of a given experiment for information/interpretation of the instructions. The idea is for the instructions to stand on their own; experimenters should note any vagaries or inconsistencies in their notes on the Data Collection sheets.

- The number of days to allot for this lesson will depend on the number of lab teams in the class and on how proficient students have become with the mechanisms being learned. Per our experience, you will definitely want to allow students to test run their own experiments and consult with you at least a day before the teams conduct one another's experiments; there are always modifications that must be made and considerations that teams have neglected to make.
- You will be collecting the Data Collection sheets as they are completed. You can review these if you like; you will be returning them to the students so that they can gather information from the experimenters prior to making their final presentations in Lesson 8. To our knowledge, we have never had an incident in which students tampered with any of the Data Collection sheets for their experiments, but if that is something you want to avoid, you can always make copies of the sheets prior to redistributing them to students.

Name:_____ Date: _____

Self-Assessment

Check the instructions of both of your experiments for the following elements. If the answer to any of the following questions is "No," then identify the step, concept, or area that is confusing you and discuss it with your teammates or the teacher, and then write down how you resolved the issue.

1. Do I have accurate and complete information pertaining to each step and all materials of the experiment? _____

2. Can I explain, in my own words, what each step is and how it contributes to the overall flow of the experiment? _____

3. Can I explain, in my own words, how each of the materials is supposed to be used in the experiment? _____

4. Can I identify the changes that are supposed to occur in the experiment? Can I explain the indicators that make me know these changes have occurred?
    _____

5. Is my experiment logical and readable? Will it make sense to the experimenters? _____

6. Have I proofread my work? _____

7. Did I cite any sources that I used appropriately? _____

8. Are my Experiment Design sheets complete? _____

9. Could somebody use my Experiment Design sheets to replicate my work?
    _____

To-Do List
1. _____
_____
2. _____
_____
3. _____
_____

Understanding Physical and Chemical Changes © Prufrock Press Inc.

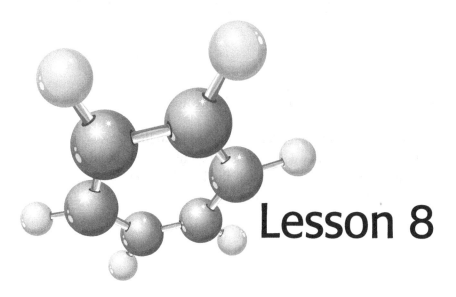

Lesson 8

Concepts

- Physical change
- Chemical change
- Scientific method
- Presentation techniques

Materials

- Final Project Rubric sheet (from Lesson 6, p. 75)
- Self-Reflection sheet (pp. 86–87)
- Completed Data Collection sheets to be redistributed to students

Student Objective

Students compile the data from the experiments they designed and consider their peers' constructive feedback. Lab groups present on their experiments.

Introduction

The teacher again reviews the final rubric and discusses the components of strong visual aids and presentations.

Recognition

In a whole-class discussion, students give examples of situations they encountered while conducting student-designed experiments. In this discussion, students use positive language and offer constructive criticism (as opposed to nitpicky feedback).

Application

Students compile data, analyze their results, and prepare to present their findings.

1. Students use the data and constructive feedback collected from their classmates to evaluate the experiments they designed. They should keep in mind the following questions, which may be posted on the board as they work: First, was the design sound and easily understood by others? And second, was the hypothesis proved successfully?

2. Students create visual aids to document and illustrate the findings of the experimenters.

Problem Solving

Students present their findings and reflect on their experiences.

1. In their lab teams, students make presentations to the class.

2. At the teacher's discretion, the class and the teacher may ask questions, offer constructive feedback, and share their experiences as experimenters. (If discussion is allowed, the presentations should be allowed to conclude first.)

3. Each team should use a visual aid to illustrate its findings for each experiment.

4. The teacher can sum up the unit by conducting a whole-class discussion and/or having students complete the Self-Reflection sheet.

Additional Notes

*   Prior to having students begin work on their presentations, you may pass back the feedback they received on their visual aids and presentations in Lesson 5.
*   Students should keep in mind the criteria listed on the Final Project Rubric sheet as they prepare a presentation evaluating their own experiments. We suggest that you ask students to discuss at least one successful element of each experiment, as well as at least one challenge that they encountered (or that experimenters encountered) in that experiment.
*   If a computer lab is available, consider coaching students to use the technology at their disposal to generate their visual aids. This can also be an enjoyable component of the unit for artistically inclined students.
*   We recommend that the first day of the lesson be dedicated to planning and reflection, and the second day to student presentations. We have found that it works best to score the rubric while presentations are in progress. Another

option is to make separate notes on the presentation, and to fill in the rubric at a later time.

- We suggest congratulating all of the students for their participation, innovation, and efforts. If it is in keeping with your school's policies, you might invite guests (other classes, administrators, and so forth) to come and view the final presentations. You might also make invitations or flyers and provide snacks.

Self-Reflection

1. What are your strengths (or what is the easiest or most exciting part) in terms of working in a lab team?

   _____

   _____

2. What are your weaknesses (or what is the most challenging part) in terms of working in a lab team?

   _____

   _____

3. Write a summary of everything you have learned about physical and chemical changes. Be sure to point out the differences between these types of changes. Use as many of the words in the box as possible (you may include additional related vocabulary if appropriate).

Data	Attributes	Scientific method
	Visual aids	Prediction
Lab safety	Phase	Indicator
	Observation	Collaborate
Size	Hypothesis	Inference
Constructive feedback		Physical change
	Shape	Conclusion
Chemical change		Experiment

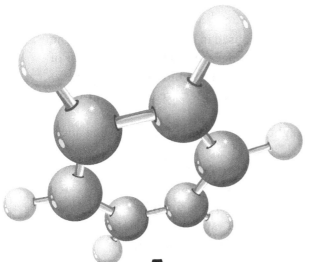

Appendix
Student Context
Rubric

The Student Context Rubric (SCR) is intended for use by the classroom teacher as a tool to help in the identification of students of masked potential. This term, *masked potential*, refers to students who are gifted, but are frequently not identified because their behaviors are not displayed to best advantage by traditional methods. The SCR was designed to be used with this series of units and the authentic performance assessments that accompany them. Although you may choose to run the units without using the SCR, you may find the rubric helpful for keeping records of student behaviors.

The units serve as platforms for the display of student behaviors, while the SCR is an instrument that teachers can use to record those behaviors when making observations. The rubric requires the observer to record the frequency of gifted behaviors, but there is also the option to note that the student demonstrates the behavior with particular intensity. In this way, the rubric is subjective and requires careful observation and consideration.

It is recommended that an SCR be completed for each student prior to the application of a unit, and once again upon completion of the unit. In this way, teachers will be reminded of behaviors to look for during the unit—particularly those behaviors that we call *loophole behaviors*, which may indicate giftedness but are often misinterpreted or overlooked. (For instance, a student's verbal ability can be missed if he or she uses it to spin wild lies about having neglected to complete an assignment.) Therefore, the SCR allows teachers to be aware of—and to document—high-ability behavior even if it is masked or used in nontraditional ways. The mechanism also provides a method for tracking changes in teachers' perceptions of their students, not only while students are working on the Interactive Discovery-Based Units for High-Ability Learners, but also while they are engaged in traditional classroom activities.

In observing student behaviors, you might consider some of the following questions after completing a lesson:

- Was there anyone or anything that surprised you today?
- Did a particular student jump out at you today?
- Did someone come up with a unique or unusual idea today?
- Was there a moment in class today when you saw a lightbulb go on? Did it involve an individual, a small group, or the class as a whole?
- In reviewing written responses after a class discussion, were you surprised by anyone (either because he or she was quiet during the discussion but had good written ideas, or because he or she was passionate in the discussion but did not write with the same passion)?
- Did any interpersonal issues affect the classroom today? If so, how were these issues resolved?
- Did the lesson go as planned today? Were there any detours?
- Is there a student whom you find yourself thinking or worrying about outside of school?
- Are there students in your classroom who seem to be on a rollercoaster of learning—"on" one day, but "off" the next?
- Are your students different outside of the classroom? In what ways are they different?
- Are there students who refuse to engage with the project?
- During a class performance, did the leadership of a group change when students got in front of their peers?
- Did your students generate new ideas today?
- What was the energy like in your class today? Did you provide the energy, or did the students?
- How long did it take the students to engage today?

Ideally, multiple observers complete the SCR for each student. If a gifted and talented specialist is available, we recommend that he or she assist. By checking off the appropriate marks to describe student behaviors, and by completing the scoring chart, participants generate quantifiable data that can be used in advocating for students who would benefit from scaffolded services. **In terms of students' scores on the SCR, we do not provide concrete cutoffs or point requirements regarding which students should be recommended for special services.** Rather, the SCR is intended to flag students for scaffolded services and to enable them to reach their potential. It also provides a way to monitor and record students' behaviors.

What follows is an explanation of the categories and items included on the SCR, along with some examples of how the specified student behaviors might be evidenced in your classroom.

Engagement

1. **Student arrives in class with new ideas to bring to the project that he or she has thought of outside of class.** New ideas may manifest themselves as ideas about how to approach a problem, about new research information found on the Internet or elsewhere outside of class, about something in the news or in the paper that is relevant to the subject, or about a connection between the subject and an observed behavior.

2. **Student shares ideas with a small group of peers, but may fade into the background in front of a larger group.** The student may rise to be a leader when the small group is working on a project, but if asked to get up in front of the class, then that student fades into the background and lets others do the talking.

3. **Student engagement results in a marked increase in the quality of his or her performance.** This is particularly evident in a student who does not normally engage in class at all. During the unit, the student suddenly becomes engaged and produces something amazing.

4. **Student eagerly interacts with appropriate questions, but may be reluctant to put things down on paper.** This is an example of a loophole behavior, or one that causes a student to be overlooked when teachers and specialists are identifying giftedness. It is particularly evident in students who live in largely "oral" worlds, which is to say that they communicate best verbally and are often frustrated by written methods, or in those who have writing disabilities.

Creativity

1. **Student intuitively makes "leaps" in his or her thinking.** Occasionally, you will be explaining something, and a lightbulb will go on for a student, causing him or her to take the concept far beyond the content being covered. Although there are students who do this with regularity, it is more often an intensity behavior, meaning that when it occurs, the student is very intense in his or her thinking, creativity, reasoning, and so on. This can be tricky to identify, because often, the student is unable to explain his or her thinking, and the teacher realizes only later that a leap in understanding was achieved.

2. **Student makes up new rules, words, or protocols to express his or her own ideas.** This can take various forms, one of which is a student's taking two words and literally combining them to try to express what he or she is thinking about. Other times, a student will want to change the rules to make his or her idea possible.

3. **Student thinks on his or her feet in response to a project challenge, to make excuses, or to extend his or her work.** This is another loophole

behavior, because it often occurs when a student is being defensive or even misbehaving, making a teacher less likely to interpret it as evidence of giftedness. It is sometimes on display during classroom debates and discussions.

4. **Student uses pictures or other inventive means to illustrate his or her ideas.** Given the choice, this student would rather draw an idea than put it into words. This could take the shape of the student creating a character web or a design idea. The student might also act out an idea or use objects to demonstrate understanding.

Synthesis

1. **Student goes above and beyond directions to expand ideas.** It is wonderful to behold this behavior in students, particularly when displayed by those students who are rarely engaged. A student may be excited about a given idea and keep generating increasingly creative or complex material to expand upon that idea. For instance, we had a student who, during the mock trial unit, became intrigued by forensic evidence and decided to generate and interpret evidence to bolster his team's case.

2. **Student has strong opinions on projects, but may struggle to accept directions that contradict his or her opinions.** This student may understand directions, but be unwilling to yield to an idea that conflicts with his or her own idea. This behavior, rather than indicating a lack of understanding, is typical of students with strong ideas.

3. **Student is comfortable processing new ideas.** This behavior is evident in students who take new ideas and quickly extend them or ask insightful questions.

4. **Student blends new and old ideas.** This behavior has to do with processing a new idea, retrieving an older idea, and relating the two to one another. For instance, a student who learns about using string to measure distance might remember making a treasure map and extrapolate that a string would have been useful for taking into account curves and winding paths.

Interpersonal Ability

1. **Student is an academic leader who, when engaged, increases his or her levels of investment and enthusiasm in the group.** This is a student who has so much enthusiasm for learning that he or she makes the project engaging for the whole group, fostering an attitude of motivation or optimism.

2. **Student is a social leader in the classroom, but may not be an academic leader.** To observe this type of behavior, you may have to be vigilant, for some students are disengaged in the classroom but come alive as soon as they cross the threshold into the hallway, where they can socialize with their

peers. Often, this student is able to get the rest of the group to do whatever he or she wants (and does not necessarily use this talent for good).

3. **Student works through group conflict to enable the group to complete its work.** When the group has a conflict, this is the student who solves the problem or addresses the issue so that the group can get back to work. This is an interpersonal measure, and thus, it does not describe a student who simply elects to do all of the work rather than confronting his or her peers about sharing the load.

4. **Student is a Tom Sawyer in classroom situations, using his or her charm to get others to do the work.** There is an important distinction to watch out for when identifying this type of behavior: You must be sure that the student is *not* a bully, coercing others to do his or her work. Instead, this student actually makes other students *want* to lend a helping hand. For instance, a twice-exceptional student who is highly talented but struggles with reading might develop charm in order to get other students to transpose his verbally expressed ideas into writing.

Verbal Communication

1. **Participation in brainstorming sessions (e.g., group work) increases student's productivity.** When this type of student is given the opportunity to verbally process with peers, he or she is often able to come up with the answer. For instance, if asked outright for an answer, this student may shrug, but if given a minute to consult with a neighbor, then the student usually is able and willing to offer the correct answer.

2. **Student constructively disagrees with peers and/or the teacher by clearly sharing his or her thoughts.** This student can defend his or her point of view with examples and reasoning—not just in a formal debate, but also in general classroom situations. He or she has learned to channel thoughts into constructive disagreement, rather than flying off the handle merely to win an argument.

3. **Student verbally expresses his or her academic and/or social needs.** This student can speak up when confused or experiencing personality clashes within a group. This student knows when to ask for help and can clearly articulate what help is needed.

4. **Student uses strong word choice and a variety of tones to bring expression to his or her verbal communication.** This student is an engaging speaker and speaks loudly and clearly enough for everybody to hear. A wide vocabulary is also indicative that this student's verbal capability is exceptional.

Student: _____

Date: _____

Fill out the rubric according to what you have observed about each student's behaviors. Then, for each area, record the number of items you marked "Not observed," "Sometimes," and "Often." Multiply these tallies by the corresponding point values (0, 1, and 2) to get the totals for each area. There is an option to check for high intensity so you can better keep track of students' behaviors.

STUDENT CONTEXT RUBRIC

ENGAGEMENT

1. Student arrives in class with new ideas to bring to the project that he or she has thought of outside of class.
   NOT OBSERVED · SOMETIMES · OFTEN · HIGH INTENSITY

2. Student shares ideas with a small group of peers, but may fade into the background in front of a larger group.
   NOT OBSERVED · SOMETIMES · OFTEN · HIGH INTENSITY

3. Student engagement results in a marked increase in the quality of his or her performance.
   NOT OBSERVED · SOMETIMES · OFTEN · HIGH INTENSITY

4. Student eagerly interacts with appropriate questions, but may be reluctant to put things down on paper.
   NOT OBSERVED · SOMETIMES · OFTEN · HIGH INTENSITY

CREATIVITY

1. Student intuitively makes "leaps" in his or her thinking.
   NOT OBSERVED · SOMETIMES · OFTEN · HIGH INTENSITY

2. Student makes up new rules, words, or protocols to express his or her own ideas.
   NOT OBSERVED · SOMETIMES · OFTEN · HIGH INTENSITY

3. Student thinks on his or her feet in response to a project challenge, to make excuses, or to extend his or her work.
   NOT OBSERVED · SOMETIMES · OFTEN · HIGH INTENSITY

4. Student uses pictures or other inventive means to illustrate his or her ideas.
   NOT OBSERVED · SOMETIMES · OFTEN · HIGH INTENSITY

SYNTHESIS

1. Student goes above and beyond directions to expand ideas.
   NOT OBSERVED · SOMETIMES · OFTEN · HIGH INTENSITY

2. Student has strong opinions on projects, but may struggle to accept directions that contradict his or her opinions.
   NOT OBSERVED · SOMETIMES · OFTEN · HIGH INTENSITY

3. Student is comfortable processing new ideas.
   NOT OBSERVED · SOMETIMES · OFTEN · HIGH INTENSITY

4. Student blends new ideas and old ideas.
   NOT OBSERVED · SOMETIMES · OFTEN · HIGH INTENSITY

INTERPERSONAL ABILITY

1. Student is an academic leader who, when engaged, increases his or her levels of investment and enthusiasm in the group.
   NOT OBSERVED · SOMETIMES · OFTEN · HIGH INTENSITY

2. Student is a social leader in the classroom, but may not be an academic leader.
   NOT OBSERVED · SOMETIMES · OFTEN · HIGH INTENSITY

3. Student works through group conflict to enable the group to complete its work.
   NOT OBSERVED · SOMETIMES · OFTEN · HIGH INTENSITY

4. Student is a Tom Sawyer in classroom situations, using his or her charm to get others to do the work.
   NOT OBSERVED · SOMETIMES · OFTEN · HIGH INTENSITY

VERBAL COMMUNICATION

1. Participation in brainstorming sessions (e.g., group work) increases student's productivity.
   NOT OBSERVED · SOMETIMES · OFTEN · HIGH INTENSITY

2. Student constructively disagrees with peers and/or the teacher by clearly sharing his or her thoughts.
   NOT OBSERVED · SOMETIMES · OFTEN · HIGH INTENSITY

3. Student verbally expresses his or her academic and/or social needs.
   NOT OBSERVED · SOMETIMES · OFTEN · HIGH INTENSITY

4. Student uses strong word choice and a variety of tones to bring expression to his or her verbal communication.
   NOT OBSERVED · SOMETIMES · OFTEN · HIGH INTENSITY

AREA	NOT 0	SOME 1	OFTEN 2	HIGH	TOTAL
ENGAGEMENT					
CREATIVITY					
SYNTHESIS					
INTERPERSONAL ABILITY					
VERBAL COMMUNICATION					
ADD TOTALS					

Developed by Cote & Blauvelt under the auspices of the Further Steps Forward Project, a Jacob Javits grant program, #S206A050086.

Understanding Physical and Chemical Changes © Prufrock Press Inc.

About the Authors

Richard G. Cote, M.B.A., is a career educator. He has dedicated 41 years to being a classroom teacher (mathematics, physics), a community college adjunct instructor (economics), a gifted and talented resource specialist, and the director of the Further Steps Forward Project, a Javits Grant program.

His development of the MESH (mathematics, English, science, and history) program has led him to several audiences. He has presented at various national conventions, civic/community groups, district school boards, teacher organizations, community colleges, and universities, and has served as a consultant to educators throughout the country. Cote helped develop the teacher certification examination for physics at the Institute for Educational Testing and Research at the University of South Florida. He completed the Florida Council on Educational Management Program in Educational Leadership, and he is the recipient of numerous awards, including a certificate of merit on economics education from the University of South Florida, a grant from the Florida Council on Economics Education, a Florida Compact award, and prestigious NAGC Curriculum Studies awards for the development of the Interactive Discovery-Based Units for High-Ability Learners series.

Now retired from the workplace, Cote continues to share his energy, creativity, and expertise with educators through the Interactive Discovery-Based Units for High-Ability Learners.

Darcy O. Blauvelt has been teaching in a variety of facilities for more than 12 years. Her educational journey has included public schools, private schools, nursery schools, and a professional theatre for children ages 3–18. Blauvelt holds educational certification in Theatre K–12, Early Childhood Education, and English Education 5–12. She holds a B.A. in theatre from Chatham College, Pittsburgh, PA, and has done graduate work at Lesley University in Massachusetts in creative arts in learning, as well as at Millersville University in Pennsylvania in psychology.

In 2005, she joined the Nashua School District as a gifted and talented resource specialist. Subsequently, she served full time as the program coordinator for the Further Steps Forward Project, a Javits Grant program, from 2005–2009. Blauvelt returned to the classroom in the fall of 2009 and currently teaches seventh-grade English in Nashua, NH. Blauvelt lives in Manchester, NH with her husband, two dogs, five cats, and the occasional son!

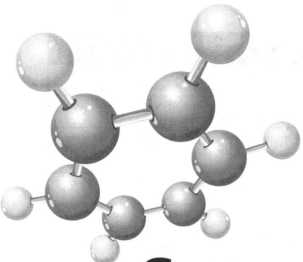

Common Core State Standards Alignment

Cluster	Common Core State Standards and Next Generation Science Standards Met
NGSS: Middle School: Matter and Its Interactions	"MS-PS1-1. Develop models to describe the atomic composition of simple molecules and extended structures.
	MS-PS1-2. Analyze and interpret data on the properties of substances before and after the substances interact to determine if a chemical reaction has occurred.
	MS-PS1-4. Develop a model that predicts and describes changes in particle motion, temperature, and state of a pure substance when thermal energy is added or removed.
	MS-PS1-5. Develop and use a model to describe how the total number of atoms does not change in a chemical reaction and thus mass is conserved.
	MS-PS1-6. Undertake a design project to construct, test, and modify a device that either releases or absorbs thermal energy by chemical processes."
NGSS: Middle School: Engineering Design	"MS-ETS1-1. Define the criteria and constraints of a design problem with sufficient precision to ensure a successful solution, taking into account relevant scientific principles and potential impacts on people and the natural environment that may limit possible solutions.
	MS-ETS1-2. Evaluate competing design solutions using a systematic process to determine how well they meet the criteria and constraints of the problem.
	MS-ETS1-3. Analyze data from tests to determine similarities and differences among several design solutions to identify the best characteristics of each that can be combined into a new solution to better meet the criteria for success.
	MS-ETS1-4. Develop a model to generate data for iterative testing and modification of a proposed object, tool, or process such that an optimal design can be achieved."

Cluster	Common Core State Standards and Next Generation Science Standards Met
CCSS ELA-Literacy: Literacy in Science/Technical Subjects (6-8)	"RST.6-8.2 Determine the central ideas or conclusions of a text; provide an accurate summary of the text distinct from prior knowledge or opinions.
	RST.6-8.3 Follow precisely a multistep procedure when carrying out experiments, taking measurements, or performing technical tasks.
	RST.6-8.5 Analyze the structure an author uses to organize a text, including how the major sections contribute to the whole and to an understanding of the topic.
	RST.6-8.6 Analyze the author's purpose in providing an explanation, describing a procedure, or discussing an experiment in a text.
	RST.6-8.8 Distinguish among facts, reasoned judgment based on research findings, and speculation in a text.
	RST.6-8.9 Compare and contrast the information gained from experiments, simulations, video, or multimedia sources with that gained from reading a text on the same topic."

Printed in the United States
by Baker & Taylor Publisher Services